All About Mummies

Dianne Irving

Contents

Mummies from Egypt

What do you know about mummies?
No, not mothers; but *mummies!*

Egypt

AFRICA

Nile

EGYPT

Egyptian mummy

Egypt is a hot, dry country in Africa.
It was the **ancient** Egyptians who made
mummies thousands of years ago.

Some ancient Egyptian
mummies were
put inside the
pyramids.

What Is a Mummy?

The ancient Egyptians wanted the bodies of people who had died to last forever. So, they **preserved** the bodies.

This is a mummy of a child.

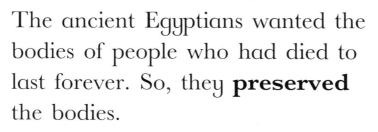

Bandages were used to wrap the body to help preserve it.

It took a long time and a lot of money to make a mummy. Only rich people like kings or queens became mummies when they died.

A statue of an
Egyptian queen.

Why Make Mummies?

The Egyptians believed that when people died, they went to the **afterlife**.

The bodies of people had to be preserved
so they would be ready for the afterlife.

These Egyptians are giving a mummy
gifts to take into the afterlife.

The Mummy-makers

Making mummies was a very special job.
The mummy-makers had to take care with all
the parts of the body.

These men are wrapping a body in
bandages to turn it into a mummy.

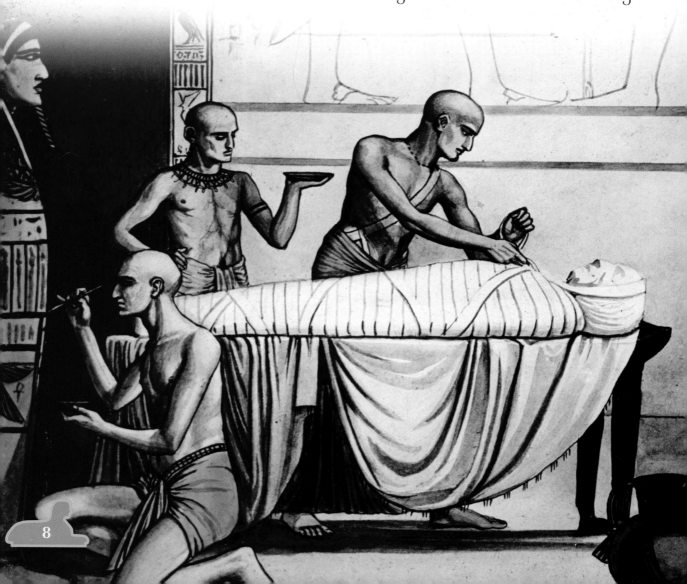

Turning a body into a mummy
took a long time.

The mummy-makers took the bodies to
a place called the Beautiful House.

A dead body at the Beautiful House

It took 70 days to make a mummy. First the body
was washed. Then the inside parts of the body were
taken out. Some of the parts were put into jars.

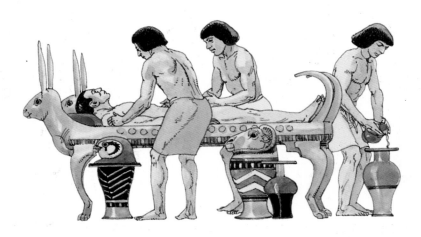

Mummy-makers washing the body

Different body parts were put in these jars with the coffins.

The mummy-makers put salt all over the body. This was to stop the body from rotting. The body was left to dry for 40 days. Then it was filled with **bandages**, salt and **spices**.

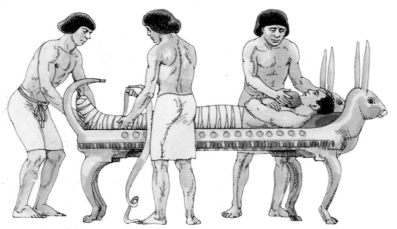

Gold, jewels and wooden tags were placed on the body to **protect** it.
The last step was to wrap the body in more bandages.

a wooden tag

The mummy-makers did such a good job that many bodies are still preserved today.

The preserved mummy is inside this coffin.

The Egyptians believed that the body would see, hear, eat and drink in the afterlife. So food and drink was left with the mummy.

These men are leaving grapes, fish and other food with the mummy to take to the afterlife.

Sometimes, the mummy had a face mask.

A mask was put on the face of the mummy to protect the body's soul from evil spirits as it made its way to the afterlife.

Homes for the Mummies

When the mummy was ready, it was put into a **sarcophagus** or **coffin**. The sarcophagus was like a home for the body in the afterlife.

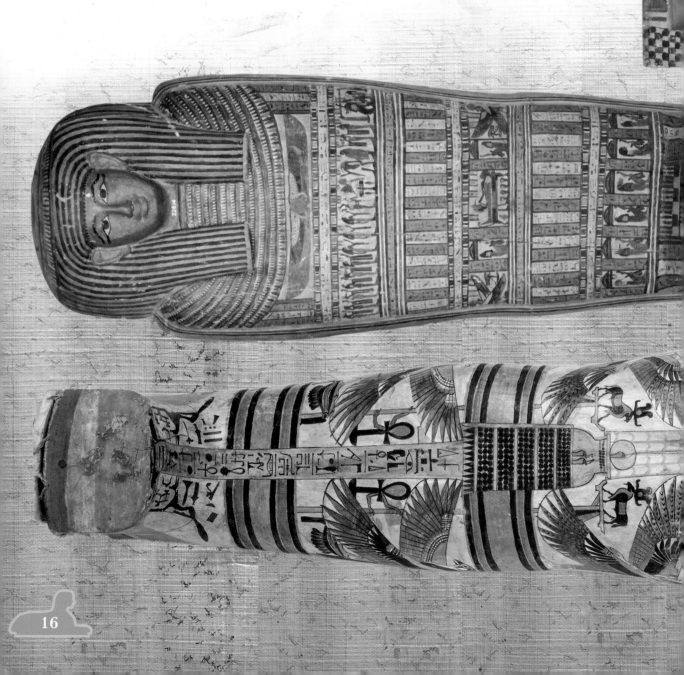

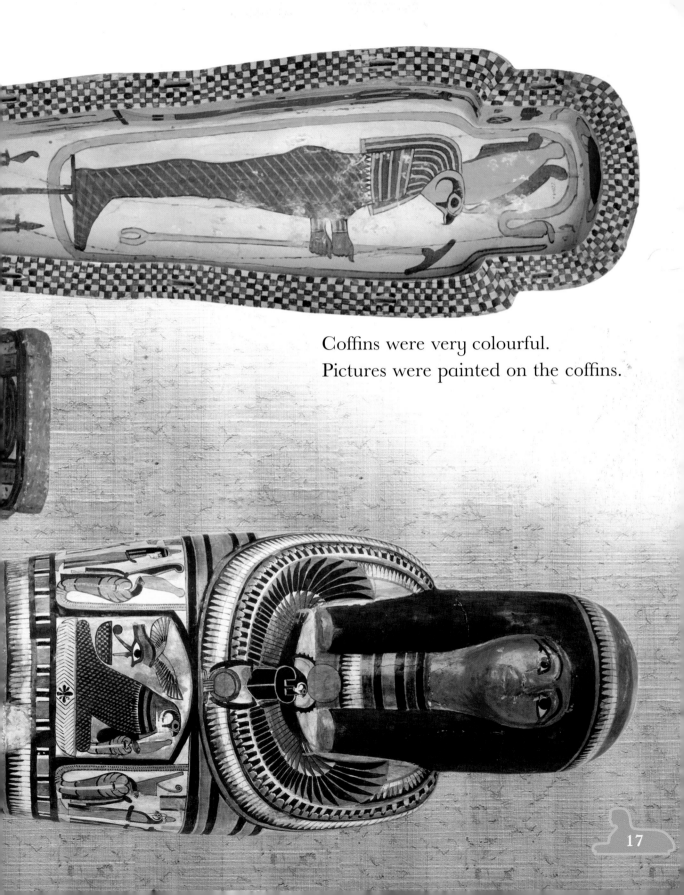

Coffins were very colourful.
Pictures were painted on the coffins.

Mummies of Kings and Queens

The kings and queens of Egypt were very important people. Some of the mummies of the kings and queens were put in gold coffins.

This is a statue of King Ramesses II who ruled Egypt from 1279 BC to 1213 BC.

The Egyptian word for king is pharaoh (say *f-air-row*). It means 'great house'.

Some of these gold coffins were put into the Great Pyramids.

King Tutankhamun

The most famous Egyptian mummy is Tutankhamun's mummy which was found in 1922. Tutankhamun (say *Toot-an-ka-moon*) was a young king. He became the king when he was 9 years old! But he died when he was 19 years old.

Tutankhamun's beautiful coffin was found in a room full of jewellery, gold chairs, musical instruments and other beautiful things.

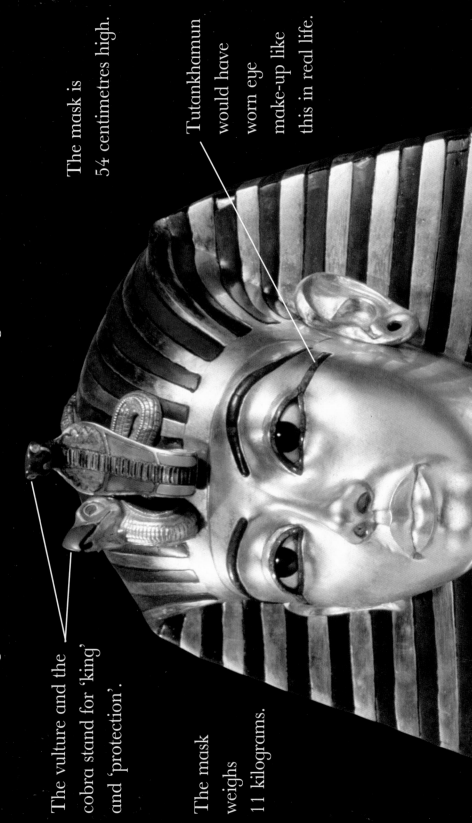

The Mask of King Tutankhamun

One of the most amazing finds was Tutankhamun's mummy mask. It was made from solid gold.

The mask is 54 centimetres high.

Tutankhamun would have worn eye make-up like this in real life.

The vulture and the cobra stand for 'king' and 'protection'.

The mask weighs 11 kilograms.

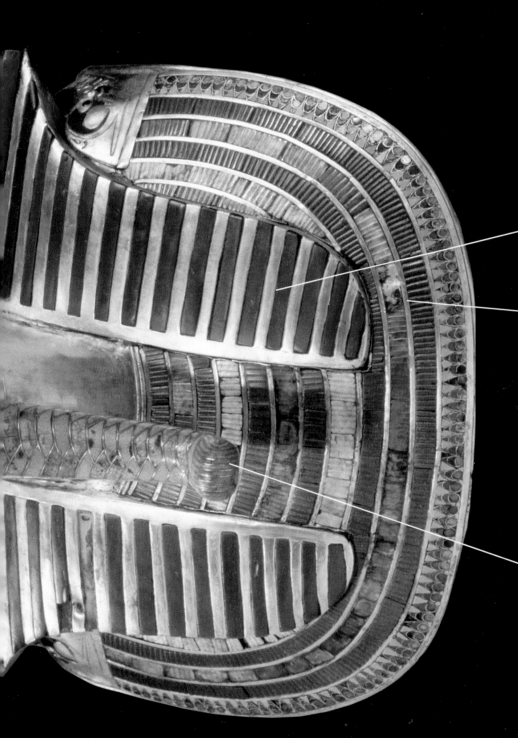

The mask's headdress is made from stripes of gold and glass that has been coloured dark blue.

The face mask's collar is decorated with gold, coloured glass and semi-precious stones.

The beard is a symbol of a king or ruler of Egypt.

Glossary

afterlife
land that you go to after you die

ancient
from a time long ago, in the past

bandages
cloth wrappings that were put around a mummy

coffin
box or case that a body is put in

preserved
stopped from rotting away

protect
keep safe, look after

sarcophagus
box or case that a body is put in

spices
food stuffs such as cinnamon